UNITED STATES COAST GUARD TRAGEDIES

By

Edward Leo Semler Jr.

Copyright © 2023 by Edward Leo Semler Jr.

All rights reserved by the author.

First Edition: 2023

Library of Congress Control Number: 2023902821

ISBN: 978-1-7376472-1-8

Printed in the United States of America

City of Publication: Schulenburg, Texas

Cover picture and layout by Edward Leo Semler Jr.

To the men and women of the U.S. Coast Guard

TABLE OF CONTENTS

Introduction	1
Station San Luis, Texas	5
U.S.C.G.C. Yamacraw	7
Lightship LV-6	9
U.S.C.G.C. Seneca	11
U.S.C.G.C. Tampa	15
U.S.C.G.C. Morrill	19
U.S.C.G.C. Lincoln	21
C.G. – 238	25
Station Manomet Point	29
Station Atlantic City	33
Lightship 117	35

Station Yaquina Bay	39
CG-V142 JF2	41
U.S.C.G.C. General Greene	43
CG-V157 J2W	45
CG-V126 RD-4	47
U.S.C.G.C. Alexander Hamilton	49
U.S.S. Wakefield	51
CG-V190 JRF-3	53
U.S.C.G.C. Muskeget	55
U.S.C.G.C. Natsek	57
C.G. – 85006	59
CG-V176 JRF-2	61
U.S.C.G.C. Escanaba	63
CG-08055 PBY-5A	65
L.S.T. - 167	67
CG-34075 JR-F	69
U.S.S. Leopold	71
U.S.S. Menges	73

U.S.C.G.C. Clover	75
L.S.T. – 327	77
U.S.C.G.C. Jackson, U.S.C.G.C. Bedloe & Lightship – 73	79
L.S.T. – 66	83
U.S.S. Callaway	85
U.S.S. Serpens	87
F.S. – 255	89
CG-32740 JSF-2	91
CG-46497 PBY-5A	93
B-17	95
CG-48284 PBY-5A	97
CG-48328 PBY-5A	99
CG-45435 PBM-5G	101
CG-055049 R50-4	103
CG-84740 PBM-5G	105
CG-46640 PBY-6A	107
CG-84738 PBM-5G	109

CG-1303 HO4S-3G	113
CG-128906 HTL-4	115
CG-2121 UF-1G	119
CG-1259 HU-16E	121
U.S.C.G.C. Triumph	123
CG-5509 HO4S-3G	129
CG-7233 HU-16E	131
CG-1363 HH-52A	133
CG-1240 HU-16E	137
CG-7237 HU-16E	139
CG-2128 HU-16E	141
U.S.C.G.C. White Alder	143
CG-1458 HH-52A	145
CG-1474 HH-3F	147
CG-2123 HU-16E	149
CG-1448 HH-52A	151
U.S.C.G.C. Cuyahoga	153
CG-1379 HH-52A	157

CG-1432 HH-3F	159
U.S.C.G.C. Blackthorn	161
CG-1471 HH-3F	165
CG-1427 HH-52A	167
CG-1420 HH-52A	169
CG-1473 HH-3F	171
U.S.C.G.C. Mesquite	173
CG-3501 E2C	175
CG-6541 HH-65	177
CG-44363 MLB	179
CG-6549 HH-65	181
CG-6505 HH-65	183
CG-1705 HC-130	185
CG-6017 MH-60T	187
CG-6535 HH-65	189
About The Author	191

INTRODUCTION

When I moved from Pennsylvania to Texas in 2015, I had to downsize. One of the things I decided to part with was the television. Ever since making that decision I have found that I have much more time to read and be more constructive. And when I want to watch something on my laptop, it tends to be educational, like researching historical events or how to fix something. To accomplish this, I tend to drift to venues like YouTube. And I even have my own channel where I upload Coast Guard and military related stuff, videos of my time in the service and vintage ones from years ago. YouTube lets me watch what I want to watch and what interests me at any given moment. Which could be German U-boats in World War I one minute, or air conditioning and refrigeration repair the next. And that's pretty much how I got the inspiration to write this book, which happens to be my tenth. I was surfing through YouTube and up pops the tragedy of the Coast Guard Cutter *Mesquite*. YouTube has a way of doing that. They monitor your viewing habits and send you videos that might interest you. So, I watched the video, which was basically a collection of evening news stories on the event. It piqued my interest and I searched for more videos that had to do with tragic events relating to the Coast Guard.

I was stationed on a Coast Guard cutter myself at the time of the *Mesquite* tragedy and it reminded me of other tragic events in Coast Guard history, such as the cutters *Tampa,* and *Blackthorn*. I decided to investigate them on the internet, and there didn't seem to be any central site or source which covered all, or least a majority, of Coast Guard tragic incidents. If there was, they either focused on sea going or aviation disasters. So, I decided to compile my own in this book.

And this is by no means a complete collection of all the tragedies that have occurred in the Coast Guard. There is a long list of those individuals who have given their life serving their country on the water, in the air, and in war & peace. But I think you will find this is a good collection of major tragedies.

I had several criteria for determining a tragic event. First, I start this book when the Revenue Cutter Service and Life-Saving Service were merged to form the United States Coast Guard on the 28th of January 1915 - Although, the Coast Guard can trace it's beginning all the way back to 1790 when the Revenue Cutter Service was founded. But I thought that was going too far back. And each one of those services could easily be broken out into their own book. Second, I decided that a tragic event was the loss of three or more Coast Guardsmen. I do make a few exceptions, like in the case of the Mesquite, in which there was no loss of life. But she was my inspiration for writing this book, so how could I leave it out.

I also do not get into speculation or assumptions about a tragedy, I simply lay out the known facts. They almost all had some sort of investigation or review board afterwards, which tried to find a cause or lay blame. And unfortunately, most of these tragedies had no survivors and the cause of their demise will never be fully known. Some have very limited information, and some are so detailed that I have included links to websites that are solely dedicated to that specific tragedy.

Although I excluded the individual loss of life stories in this book, I often ponder the ones that I remember. The MK3 who lost his life on the *CGC Chase* in the mid 1980's in an engine room fire, on a seemingly routine patrol. The SN who fell to his death in the late 1990's on *CGC Eagle* completing simple maintenance up in the main mast. The *CGC Dependable* shipmate that transferred and committed suicide. Their stories will always be with me. And I am sure you have your own list of tragedies.

In the following pages you will read about tragic events detailing life and death. And for the most part fit into the unofficial Coast Guard motto "You have to go out, but you don't have to return."

STATION SAN LUIS
STATION GALVESTON
STATION VELASCO

16 August 1915 – Hurricanes are no strangers to south Texas, but in 1915 the storm was so intense that it swept away Coast Guard Stations San Luis, Galveston, and Velasco.

Due to the limited news service at the time, reports were as high as twelve crewmembers lost at Station San Luis. But the total loss was eventually reduced to only four crew members. One of the crewmembers recounted being in the water, floating and swimming for over forty hours and traveling thirty miles.

"My wife was with me and several members of the San Luis crew in the station lifeboat when the storm broke Monday night. We thought we would be safe in the boat as it was moored to the station. All of us had on life-preservers. Suddenly my wife was pitched forward by a quick, violent gust of wind, and I reached out to grasp her, and slipped and fell overboard. It was impossible for me to swim back to the boat or to get to shore in that hurricane, so I just alternated swimming and floating, the life preserver helped me to keep afloat when I felt exhausted. I swam as much as possible to keep my blood circulating and to keep as warm as I could in the water. Finally, I managed to reach shore near Texas City Wednesday morning and was almost exhausted. I have been unable to get any word of the fate of my wife."

The crewmember and his wife had only been married twenty days. And unfortunately, the boat she was in capsized, and she did not survive. Four other crewmembers of San Luis Station in the boat also perished.

Although swept away, the station at Galveston did not lose any of its crewmembers.

And Station Velasco lost two Crewmembers.

In total, six Coast Guardsmen were killed in the hurricane.

Sources

Evening Star 19 Aug 1915

www.cgemf.org

Fort Worth Record – Telegram 22 August 1915

The Houston Post 23 Aug 1915

U.S.C.G.C. YAMACRAW

03 March 1917 – Coast Guard Cutter *Yamacraw* was a 191' vessel homeported out of Savannah, Georgia.

The American tanker *Louisiana* was enroute from Port Arthur, Texas to Marcus Hook, Pennsylvania when she grounded herself on Little Gull Shoals off Ocean City, Maryland. Crews from Coast Guard Stations Ocean City and Isle of Wight made two trips out to *Louisiana* to offer assistance and remove the crew. But the *Louisiana* turned down assistance and said they were in no danger.

The *Yamacraw* was enjoying liberty in Norfolk, Virginia when she was dispatched to assist a vessel off Metompkin Inlet, Virginia. Leaving over half of her enlisted crew in Norfolk, she got underway, probably thinking she would be right back.

While underway she was diverted to assist the *Louisiana*.

They reached Little Gull Shoals around 1900 and once on scene *Yamacraw* launched a small boat with nine crewmembers to go over to the *Louisiana,* which capsized on the way in the rough seas. A second small boat with two crewmembers was sent to assist the capsized first boat, and it also capsized. And yet a third boat was sent over with four men, and it capsized.

The capsizing's left ten of *Yamacraw*'s crew dead, all from the first two boats sent over. The lone survivor was from the second boat who clung to a keg and was washed ashore. The four on the third boat were rescued by one of the nearby Coast Guard Stations. With not enough crewmembers to do anything else, *Yamacraw* stood off as other vessels came out to assist the *Louisiana*.

U.S.C.G.C. Yamacraw

Sources

The Philadelphia Inquirer 06 March 1917

www.navsource.org – picture of *Yamacraw*

LIGHTSHIP LV-6

05 February 1918 – Coast Guard *Lightship LV-6* was also referred to as Cross Rip Lightship. She was stationed at the Cross Rip Station about twelve miles north of Nantucket Island in Nantucket Sound and about midway between the islands of Nantucket and Martha's Vineyard.

Lightships were basically floating lighthouses used to mark navigation. Once in place they anchored to stay on station.

A heavy ice flow ripping her from her anchorage and the crew of six Coast Guardsmen aboard *LV-6* were being carried helplessly towards open water. *LV-6* didn't have any mast, sails, or wireless equipment and was at the mercy of the sea state as she drifted helplessly in open water.

Rescue ships from Woods Hole, Massachusetts and Navy vessels from Newport, Rhode Island went in search of *LV-6*. They searched for weeks without ever locating *LV-6* or her crew.

The six Coast Guardsmen on *LV-6* were all presumed dead.

Cross Rip Lighthouse LV-6

Sources

The Boston Globe 06 February 1918

www.archives.uslhs.org – picture of *LV-6*

U.S.C.G.C. SENECA

16 September 1918 – Coast Guard Cutter *Seneca* was a 204' vessel conducting convoy duty in World War I.

At the start of World War I, in 1914, the United States remained neutral - and there was no United States Coast Guard. It would be another year, in 1915, that the United States Revenue Cutter Service and the United States Lifesaving Service would be joined to form the United States Coast Guard. And a few years later America was pulled into the war to end all wars in 1917. And with the declaration of war came the transfer of six Coast Guard cutters to the U.S. Navy. These six cutters, *Seneca* being one of them, were to operate in European waters conducting convoy duty.

Convoy duty for these cutters consisted mainly of escorting vessels loaded with men, equipment, and supplies back and forth across the English Channel. During this time enemy submarines, predominantly German, were the main threat.

While escorting a convoy to Gibraltar one of those vessel's, the *Wellington*, was torpedoed about 300 miles from their destination. Although having her bow blown off, she remained afloat. Seneca arrived on scene and chased off the submarine before she could finish *Wellington* off.

Thinking they could keep *Wellington* afloat and sail to France, eleven of her crew and nineteen of *Seneca's* crew volunteered to try and sail her to safety. Needing to rejoin the much larger convoy, *Seneca* steamed off and left *Wellington* to limp to France.

After about twelve hours *Wellington's* forward bulkhead gave way and she sank. As she went down, she took men with her, men jumped into the water, and some got in the lone lifeboat. In the end eleven *Seneca* and five *Wellington* crewmembers lost their lives.

Reading the numerous American newspaper articles about the event, there are several that described heroics from their hometown boys serving on *Seneca*. All the *Seneca* crewmembers who volunteered to go over to *Wellington* were awarded medals for their bravery.

I had the privilege to sail on a namesake of *Seneca* in the 1980's, *Seneca WMEC-906*, where the heroics of her 1918 crew were well known.

Sources

The Evening World 23 September 1918

www.wikipedia.org

www.navsource.org – picture of *Seneca*

U.S.C.G.C. Seneca

U.S.C.G.C. TAMPA

26 September 1918 - Coast Guard Cutter *Tampa* was a 190' vessel conducting convoy duty just like *Seneca* in the previous story.

In the following picture, which is the last known photograph of *Tampa*, it stated she is anchored in the Bristol Channel in southern England.

Tampa in the Bristol Channel

On the 26th of September *Tampa* delivered a convoy into the Irish Sea from their departure point of Gibraltar. After completing their safe passage, she was directed to Milford Haven in Wales to refuel. As she was transiting the Bristol Channel alone at sunset, *Tampa* was spotted by *UB-91*, a German submarine. Firing a single torpedo *UB-91* hit the *Tampa* and she exploded, killing all on board.

The following picture is a painting by John D. Wisinski and shows *UB-91* with *Tampa* exploding.

UB-91 and *Tampa* exploding

The painting however is not realistic. *UB-91* was submerged when she attacked *Tampa*, she fired the torpedo from her aft tube, and she was over 550 meters away. But it gets the point across.

The number of crewmembers killed differs from several different sources. *Tampa* had a normal complement of 70 crewmembers, but her war time compliment was higher, and I will use the figure of 111 killed, which is given on the Coast Guards official website. Other sources list higher numbers which include an estimated 16 additional British naval and civilian personnel.

Out of an estimated 127 personnel onboard only three bodies were recovered from the *Tampa*. Two had washed ashore in Lamphey, Wales and one was picked up by a British patrol boat. The loss of the *Tampa* and crew was the single biggest tragedy for the Coast Guard in World War 1.

The two bodies that washed ashore in Lamphey were buried in the local church cemetery by the church parishioners. Of the two, one was able to be identified. The crewmember that was able to be identified was later moved back to the United States by his family. The other unknown *Tampa* crewmember was left in his Lamphey grave, marked with a headstone provided by the church. And the church has faithfully taken care of the unknown *Tampa* crewmen's grave to this day.

Tampa, as I had mentioned earlier, was alone when she was attacked. So, there was no witness to what fate had come to her. All that was known at the time was that there was a large explosion in her general direction. And it was speculated that she was torpedoed by a submarine. That speculation was confirmed less than two months later when *UB-91* surrendered to Britain. Her log books detailed the attack and sinking of *Tampa* with a single torpedo.

The commanding officer of *UB-91* is said to have witnessed a second explosion immediately after the initial torpedo explosion. After 15 minutes he surfaced to look for survivors, but nothing and no one was visible.

Once again, the story of the *Tampa* was well known to me before researching it for this book. I had served on her second namesake, *Tampa WHEC-902* as the main propulsion chief in the late 1990's.

Sources

Charles R. Haberlein - picture of *Tampa*

www.thepatriotfiles.com

Military Times 22 September 2018

U.S.C.G.C. MORRILL

16 November 1925 – Coast Guard Cutter *Morrill* was a 145' vessel and changing homeports from Detroit, Michigan to Boston, Massachusetts where she would enforce Prohibition laws

While transiting from Detroit to Boston *Morrill* anchored off Sandy Point, five miles from Shelburne, Nova Scotia. After a day at shore, nine of the crew were heading back to *Morrill* in the cutters 26' sailboat. While making the transit the seas picked up and the sailboat was caught in a squall. The boat tipped on its side and the crew tried to cut away the rigging and right the boat, but it capsized, and the nine men were thrown into the icy water. Five managed to reach the slippery keel of the overturned boat and clung to it. The other four held onto the edges.

The lone survivor said that he went crazy watching his shipmates slip one by one into the freezing water and drift away. Finally, after the last of his shipmates had drifted away, the lone survivor started to swim to shore, where he arrived safely.

Eight Coast Guardsmen lost their lives.

U.S.C.G.C. Morrill

Sources

Bartlesville Examiner-Enterprise 17 November 1925
www.navsource.org – picture of *Morrill*

U.S.C.G.C. LINCOLN

18 December 1926 – Coast Guard Cutter *Lincoln* was a very interesting cutter. She was a Rum Runner, this is of course being in Prohibition times, and confiscated by the government. She was then converted to a Coast Guard cutter and was being used as a supply ship.

Homeported out of Cape May, New Jersey *Lincoln* with her crew of seven were on their way to Baltimore, Maryland with a load of scrap metal. From there they would go to Moorehead City, North Carolina and pick up a load of metal to bring back to Cape May.

Off the coast of North Carolina, several miles southwest of *Cape Lookout* Lightship, *Lincoln* caught fire and burned to the water line, and sank.

A passing British steamer, the *Defender*, picked up the lone *Lincoln* survivor.

The commander of the Coast Guard facility at Cape May held out hope for the remaining six. "Until their bodies are found I will not believe that they will not reappear. The ship caught fire only two miles from the lightship and I believe that they managed to get aboard it. The lightship is not equipped with radio apparatus during this season of the year, consequently I believe that is why they have not been heard from. If an explosion preceded the fire, I believe that the cutters now searching the wreckage will pick up the men. That kind of a wreck always leaves plenty of wreckage and Lincoln was a wood ship."

But in the end, the six Coast Guardsmen had perished.

Sources

Zanesville Times Signal 19 December 1926

www.naval-history.net – picture of *Lincoln*

U.S.C.G.C. Lincoln

CG-238

20 February 1927 – Coast Guard *238* was a 75' patrol boat assigned to Provincetown, Massachusetts.

A huge storm had barreled down on the eastern seaboard causing incredible damage. *CG-238* was anchored about three miles off Cape Cod trying to ride the storm out. As the storm ponded the small patrol boat, Coast Guardsmen from Station Highland saw light signals from *CG-238* stating she was in distress. The message was relayed to Coast Guard Base 5 in Boston. They dispatched two Coast Guard Cutters and two Naval vessels to assist.

As a passenger liner steamed past *CG-238* the Coast Guardsmen on land tried to signal her to assist *CG-238*, but she probably didn't see the signal or *CG-238* in the heavy seas as she continued without stopping.

The Coast Guardsmen on land readied their boats and guns with breeches buoys in hopes of maybe attempting a rescue. But the storm was too much for such an attempt.

As the storm raged, the signals form *CG-238* stopped. Their fellow Coast Guardsmen on shore thought that may have meant that *CG-238* was out of danger. Then the heavy seas tore *CG-*

238 from her anchorage and the Coast Guardsmen on shore watched as *CG-238* was thrown on the beach at High Head. The storm continued to slam the boat down, rolling it over and over.

Two bodies emerged from the heavy waves, which were quickly picked up by their fellow Coast Guardsmen before being reclaimed by the seas.

The crew of eight were all killed.

Sources

York Daily Record 21 February 1927

www.lighthouseantiques.net – picture of 75'

Coast Guard 75' Patrol Boat

STATION MANOMET POINT

10 March 1928 – Coast Guard Station Manomet Point is located at Plymouth, Massachusetts.

The passenger ship *SS Robert E Lee,* with its 263 passengers and crew had run aground off Station Manomet Point in a huge storm. The grounding wasn't a surprise to the Coast Guard Station, their watchman having seen it headed for danger. After notifying Coast Guard Command in Boston, the station's crew made numerous attempts to get their 30' small boat into the water and past the breaking seas, but each time they were thrown back.

The following day, with a call from the *SS Robert E Lee* to the station – "Can you send your boat?" The reply from the station was – "We will try." And the station was able to send out a rescue boat with eight Coast Guardsmen and a volunteer. A Boston Globe reporter and photographer were at the station, and you can see the rescue boat leaving in the last picture in this chapter.

The boat made it to the *SS Robert E Lee,* sending several men aboard to coordinate rescue plans. As they were returning to shore, the 30' boat capsized in the heavy waves, sending its crew into the sea. A large crowd had gathered on the beach to watch and assist in the rescue and looked on in horror as the boat and men were tossed into the water. All they could do was wait until they were washed ashore. And when they did make it, some were lifeless. The seas had claimed the lives of three Coast Guardsmen.

The crew and passengers were all safely rescued from the *SS Robert E Lee* by Coast Guard cutters and other assets and transferred to another vessel, the *SS George Washington*.

For a really detailed article on this tragedy, with pictures of the crew, please reference the Boston Globe article at the end of this chapter.

SS Robert E Lee off Station Manomet Point

Station Manomet Point going out in their 30' boat that would eventually capsize

Sources

Boston Globe 10 March 1928 – article and pictures

STATION ATLANTIC CITY

06 March 1932 – Coast Guard Station Atlantic City was located at Atlantic City, New Jersey.

A huge storm had hit the eastern seaboard and the Coast Guard had numerous assets out assisting those in distress. With freezing temperatures and snow falling, a small boat with a three-man crew left Station Atlantic City to assist a skiff about 10 miles out at sea. There was no sign of the skiff so they returned to the station.

While the first boat was out looking for the skiff, a second boat with three crewmen was sent from the station to assist the sloop *Anna*.

When the second boat failed to return to the station, the first boat with a crew of three went out looking for them. They didn't locate the second boat and were heading back into the station when their motor cut out on them just off Heinz Pier. With no power, the freezing sea tossed them until they capsized. The three Coast Guardsmen grabbed onto the overturned boat and people from the pier threw them lifelines. One of the Coast Guardsmen grabbed a line, was tossed by the sea, let loose, and was washed ashore barely alive. Another grabbed a line, was almost to the pier when he let loose. His last words – "God! I can't hold on any longer." And he drowned. The third was never able to grab a line and drowned.

The men from the second boat were never found. In all, five Coast Guardsmen were killed.

Sources

Courier-Post 07 March 1932

LIGHTSHIP 117

15 May 1934 – Coast Guard *Lightship 117*, also known as the *Nantucket Lightship*, was similar to that of the *Cross Rip Lightship* in a previous chapter.

While transiting in heavy fog the passenger liner *Olympic* collided with the *117,* which was at anchor, and put out the following messages "Have sunk *Nantucket Lightship*, am standing by to pick up crew" and then "Please inform all concerned that have been in collision with *Nantucket lightship* and have sunk same. Standing by saving crew."

A later message sent by the *Olympic* to its owners, and intercepted by the Coast Guard at Woods Hole, Massachusetts gave a brief explanation as to what happened.

The captain of the *Olympic* stated that the collision occurred on an angle. When the crash appeared inevitable, the captain ordered full speed astern, but they smashed into *117* between her masts and she immediately sank with her fog siren still blowing loudly. Passengers on *Olympic* were in a panic and rushed to the decks to see what was happening.

The *Olympic* then put over her lifeboats to rescue the eleven-man crew of *117*. She managed to pick up seven, the other four drowned. But unfortunately, out of the seven rescued, three later died.

In total, seven Coast Guardsmen were killed in the collision.

U.S.C.G. Lightship 117

Sources

The Ottawa Journal 15 May 1934

www.nelights.com – picture of *Lightship 117*

Painting of *Olympic* colliding with *Lightship 117*

STATION YAQUINA BAY

26 February 1935 – Coast Guard Station Yaquina Bay is located at the mouth of Yaquina Bay, Oregon.

A barge with a clamshell digger was being towed by a tug from Astoria, Oregon to Florence, Oregon. As it was passing Yaquina Bay in 40' seas the barge started to take on water. The tug cut the barge loose and it grounded on the jetty leading into Yaquina Bay. The tug fearing for the two crewmembers on the barge called for help.

Coast Guard Station Yaquina Bay sent a boat with a crew of five to assist. As the Coast Guard boat neared the barge, it swung to close, got entangled in wreckage from the barge, and capsized. The five Coast Guardsmen were thrown into the water. Two eventually made it to the jetty, suffering from hypothermia and minor injuries. The other three Coast Guardsmen drowned.

Sources

Arizona Republic 27 February 1935

CG-V142 JF2

15 June 1936 – Coast Guard *V142* was a Grumman JF-2 Duck single propeller aircraft assigned to Air Station St. Petersburg, Florida.

The aircraft took off from its air station in search of two boys who had gone missing the previous day while fishing. Assisting in the search was the *CG-193*, a 110' boat. Several hours after take-off *V142* spotted the missing boys who were alive and had tied their boat to a range light off Pinellas Point. *V142* radioed this information back to the Operations Center at the air station and circled over the boys while directing *CG-193* to their location.

While in a right turn *V142* suddenly plunged into the water at a high rate of speed, killing the three-man crew. The York Daily News-Times called it the worst ariel disaster in Coast Guard History. It was reported that *CG-193* reached the plane, attached a grappling hook, but no bodies were recovered. But another source stated the bodies were later recovered.

All three Coast Guardsmen were killed.

Grumman JF2

Sources

www.check-six.com

The York Daily News Times 15 June 1936

Portage Daily Register 15 June 1936

U.S.C.G.C. GENERAL GREENE

21 September 1938 – Coast Guard Cutter *General Greene* was 125' in length and homeported out of Boston, Massachusetts.

A strong 80 mph hurricane had hit the New England coast and Coast Guard assets were deployed to assist the many vessels caught out at sea and inland flooding. The *General Greene* was assigned to assist in the vicinity of Woods Hole, Massachusetts. During the operation three crewmembers were washed overboard by the heavy seas and drowned. It is unclear if the bodies were recovered.

The tragedy didn't slow the *General Greene* down, and soon after losing three crewmembers she picked up two persons from a roof top and brought them aboard.

U.S.C.G.C. General Greene

Sources

Evening Star 22 September 1938

Painting of General Greene by William Ravell

CG-V157 J2W

19 December 1938 – Coast Guard *V157* was a Waco J2W single propeller aircraft assigned to the Air Patrol Detachment El Paso, Texas and flew out of Floyd Bennett Field.

The aircraft was enroute to a final destination of Houston, with a scheduled stop at Kelly Field in San Antonio. The aircraft had four crewmembers, the pilot and co-pilot occupied the front seat and the two others in the back seat.

While transiting the plane crashed near Boerne, Texas. The first person on the scene was the local Justice of the Peace who lived only 100 yards away from the plane's impact. He said wreckage was scattered over two acres and the plane was broken in two. The pilot's body, who was also the commanding officer of the Coast Guard Detachment at El Paso, was found wrapped in his parachute at the crash scene along with the two passengers. The co-pilot was found several yards from the others.

There was no known cause of the crash, and all four Coast Guardsmen were killed.

Waco J2W

Sources

El Paso Times 20 December 1938

www.cgaviationhistory.org

CG-V126 RD-4

05 August 1941 – Coast Guard *V126* was a Douglas RD-4 Dolphin twin propeller aircraft assigned to Air Station San Francisco, California.

The crew of three took off from their air station conducting a normal patrol of the Farallon Islands, which are 26 miles southwest of the Golden Gate Bridge. While enroute *V126* flew into the typical fog found in the San Francisco area. When they did not make their regularly scheduled radio check, a search was conducted for them. The fog slowed the search progress, but eventually the remains of *V126* were spotted in the water 500 yards south of the Farallon Islands.

By the time a Coast Guard cutter and Navy mine sweeper could make it to the scene, they were only able to recover one body and some parts of the wreckage.

It's thought that *V126* was flying low due to the fog and struck rocks sticking up from the Farallon Islands.

All three Coast Guardsmen were killed.

Douglas RD-4

Sources

www.check-six.com

U.S.C.G.C. ALEXANDER HAMILTON

29 January 1942 – Coast Guard Cutter *Alexander Hamilton* was a 327' cutter conducting convoy duty during World War II.

As *Alexander Hamilton* was heading to Iceland, she was diverted to assist the vessel *Yukon (AF-9)* who was disabled. Along with the *Gwin (DD-433)* the three vessels headed for Reykjavik, Iceland. As they neared their destination German submarine *U-132* fired off four torpedoes at *Alexander Hamilton*, hitting her in the side with one. The hit was in a critical location causing extensive flooding and explosions from her engine room.

Twenty-six Coast Guardsmen aboard *Alexander Hamilton* were killed in the initial and subsequent explosions that followed. Eighty-three crewmembers were able to abandon ship and were picked up and transported to Reykjavik.

Still afloat, *Alexander Hamilton* was deemed a navigation hazard and eventually sunk with the assistance of allied vessels firing on her.

Due to war time censorship, the story of *Alexander Hamilton* being torpedoed and later sunk was not reported until the 23rd of February 1942.

U.S.C.G.C. Alexander Hamilton

Sources

www.history.uscg.mil – article and picture

U.S.S. WAKEFIELD

30 January 1942 – *U.S.S. Wakefield* was a 705' Navy troop transport ship manned with Coast Guard personnel during World War II.

While refueling in Keppel Harbor, Singapore *Wakefield* was hit by a bomb dropped by a Japanese plane. It exploded killing four Coast Guardsmen.

U.S.S. Wakefield

CG-V190 JRF-3

16 April 1942 – Coast Guard *V190* was a Grumman JRF-3 twin propeller aircraft assigned to Air Station Brooklyn, New York.

During a test flight of *V190* the crew of three were diverted off Nantucket to search for an enemy submarine. As they searched, the weather began to worsen, and it was getting dark. The plane never returned and was never heard from again.

The Coast Guard Third District believed that *V190* crashed in the vicinity of Gay Head on Martha's Vineyard because one of the crewmembers washed ashore there. The other two crewmembers and the plane were never found.

All Three Coast Guardsmen were killed in the crash.

Grumman JRF-3

Sources

www.cgaviationhistory.org - picture

The Bellingham Harald 17 April 1942

www.check-six.com

U.S.C.G.C. MUSKEGET

09 September 1942 – Coast Guard Cutter *Muskeget (WAG-48)* was a 233' vessel homeported out of Boston, Massachusetts. She was assigned to weather patrol duty in the North Atlantic.

Deploying on her second weather patrol, she arrived on station at the southern tip of Greenland. While on patrol she was presumed lost with all One Hundred sixteen Coast Guardsmen, one Public Health Service Officer and Four Civilians when she was never heard from again.

It wasn't until after the war that records indicated German submarine *U-755* had torpedoed her. It was the first patrol for *U-755* and the first ship she had sunk. According to records from *U-755* she is said to have surfaced after sinking *Muskeget* and saw two life rafts with men aboard. It was logged that the survivors were thought to have yelled "*Muskeget*." *U-755* submerged and did not assist.

U.S.C.G.C. Muskeget

Sources

www.wikipedia.org

United States Navy - picture

U.S.C.G.C. NATSEK

17 December 1942 – Coast Guard Cutter *Natsek* was a 116' vessel homeported in Boston, Massachusetts. She was a converted wooden hulled fishing vessel used in the Greenland Patrols during World War II.

Returning with two other vessels to Boston, *Natsek* and the small convoy left Narsarsuaq, Greenland. After transiting the open waters of the Labrador Sea, the vessels had separated, although *Natsek* and another vessel were still together and began to transit the Strait of Belle Isle, Newfoundland.

The weather was bad and both vessels were experiencing severe icing. They eventually lost contact with each other and the *Natsek* never arrived in Boston. Her crew of twenty-four Coast Guardsmen were presumed lost and the *Natsek* and her crew were never found.

U.S.C.G.C. Natsek

Sources

www.history.uscg.mil – article and picture

C.G. - 85006

27 March 1943 – Coast Guard *85006* was an 85' private yacht converted into a patrol boat for use during World War II.

Setting out from Coast Guard Station Manasquan, New Jersey the crew of ten aboard *85006* were heading out to her patrol area. *85006* was assigned to coastal patrol duties and carried depth chargers. While enroute she experienced engine problems. After resolving the casualty on the fuel system, she resumed her patrol. The following morning there was a large explosion leaving five crewmembers still alive and clinging to various pieces of wreckage floating in the water.

By the time help arrived six hours later, there was only one survivor. The lone survivor said that he had smelled gasoline fumes before the explosion.

In all, nine Coast Guardsmen were killed.

C.G.- 85006

Sources

www.njscuba.net – picture

www.ibiblio.org

CG-V176 JRF-2

06 April 1943 – Coast Guard *V176* was a Grumman JRF-2 twin propeller aircraft assigned to Air Station Port Angeles, Washington.

Very little is known surrounding the crash of *V176* and her crew of four. Possibly because of war time censorship the papers only mention it twice and limited their coverage to only a paragraph. What is known is that they took off from their air station and afterwards the residents of Blyn, Washington heard an impact up on Blyn Mountain. Rescue crews arrived and found that *V176* had crashed into the side of the mountain. The pilot and co-pilot were killed on impact, but two crewmembers survived. They were brought off the mountain, but later died of their injuries.

All four Coast Guardsmen were killed in the crash.

Sources

www.check-six.com

U.S.C.G.C. ESCANABA

13 June 1943 - Coast Guard Cutter *Escanaba (WPG-77)* was a 165' cutter with a complement of 105 crewmembers. She was detailed to the Greenland Patrol and primarily transited in the North Atlantic.

On 10 June 1943 *Escanaba* commenced escorting a convoy from Narsarssuak, Greenland to St. John's Newfoundland. At around 0510 on the 13th the other vessels in the convoy saw a large flash in the direction of *Escanaba*, but no explosion was heard. Two other Coast Guard vessels in the convoy rushed over to investigate. After only 10 minutes from sighting the flash, the vessels were on scene. But all they managed to pick up were two survivors and one body from the frigid 39° water. The remaining 103 crewmembers were never recovered.

It is still unknown what caused *Escanaba* to sink so fast, like *Tampa* in World War I. No enemy submarine claimed sinking her. And the general theory is that she either hit a submerged mine that was adrift or an explosion in her magazine from a depth charge.

U.S.C.G.C Escanaba (WPG-77)

UCG-08055 PBY-5A

18 July 1943 – Coast Guard *08055* was a Consolidated PBY-5A 2 twin propeller aircraft assigned to Air Station San Francisco, California.

The crew of four Coast Guardsmen and four passengers took off for a camara mapping survey over Alaska. The special camera they carried could photograph 313 square miles at a height of 21,780 feet.

While conducting the survey *08055* crashed into Mount Moffat near Adak, Alaska.

The four Coast Guardsmen and four passengers were all killed.

Sources

www.cgaviationhistory.org – picture of PBY-5A

www.check-six.com - picture of crash

Coast Guard PBY-5A

Crash site of *08055* on Mount Moffat

L.S.T. - 167

25 September 1943 – *Landing Ship Tank -167* was a 327' vessel operated by the Coast Guard during World War II.

While operating at Ruravai Beach on the island of Vella Lavella, which is part of the Solomon Islands, *L.S.T.-167* was attacked by Japanese aircraft. The bombing caused severe damage to *167*. The figures on the number of Coast Guardsmen wounded, killed, and missing in the attack vary from sources. But numbers hover around twenty wounded and fifteen killed or missing in action.

Landing Ship Tank

Sources

www.media.defense.gov

www.nps.gov

CG-34075 JRF-5

19 November 1943 – Coast Guard *34075* was a Grumman JRF-2 twin propeller aircraft stationed at Port Angeles, Washington.

The aircraft was assigned to operate in Alaska on special duty out of Kodiak Island. *34075* had taken off from Port Heiden into a low cloud ceiling and icy conditions. After getting airborne she radioed the airfield that the weather was too bad and they were heading back. The plane ended up crashing and along with her crew was unable to be recovered. Due to the lack of documentation, it is unknown if the plane was even found at the time of the crash.

The crash site was eventually discovered in 1949, but rough terrain prevented recovery and the site was once again lost. Finally in 1987 a Wildlife Refuge official came across the site 40 miles northeast of Port Heiden and the crew's remains were recovered.

Three Coast Guardsmen were killed in the crash.

Sources

www.check-six.com

www.upi.com

U.S.S. LEOPOLD

09 March 1944 – *U.S.S. Leopold (DE-319)* was a 306' Navy destroyer escort manned with a Coast Guard crew. She was assigned to escort duty during World Warr II.

While escorting a convoy south of Iceland she reported a radar contact indicating an enemy submarine was nearby. *Leopold* was ordered to break from the convoy and attack the submarine along with another Coast Guard manned destroyer, the *Joyce*.

As *Leopold* came in for the attack, German submarine *U-255* fired off a torpedo which stuck *Leopold*. The torpedo hit caused extensive damage to *Leopold* and her crew started to abandon ship in the freezing water. She soon broke in two. Luckily, *Joyce* was nearby and assisted in rescue efforts, although she was having to deal with *U-255,* who was still looking for another target.

Joyce managed to pick up twenty-eight survivors. One hundred and seventy-one Coast Guardsmen were killed.

I could not find a good picture of *Leopold.* But did find one of *Joyce*, which is a sister ship.

U.S.S. Joyce (DE-317)

Sources

www.history.navy.mil

www.desausa.org – picture

U.S.S. MENGES

03 May 1944 – *U.S.S. Menges (DE-320)* was a 306' Navy destroyer escort manned with a Coast Guard crew and was a sister ship to *Leopold* and *Joyce*. She was also assigned to escort duty during World Warr II.

While escorting a convoy she detected a submarine radar contact and moved in to attack. The German submarine *U-371* got off her torpedo first and hit *Menges* aft, destroying the back part of the ship. *Menges* managed to stay afloat and was towed into Bougie, Algeria.

Menges lost thirty-one Coast Guardsmen with twenty-five wounded.

Sources

www.history.navy.mil

www.navsource.org – starboard profile picture

www.reddit.com – before and after picture

U.S.S. Menges (DE-320)

Left - Before & Right - After torpedo hit

U.S.C.G.C. CLOVER

18 May 1944 – Coast Guard Cutter *Clover* was a 180' buoy tender and assigned to LORAN construction duties in Alaska.

While operating near Dry Bay, Alaska *Clover* was called to assist two fishing vessels in distress, the *Loangen* and the *Alaskan*, which had grounded themselves in the Bay. *Clover* launched a small boat with a crew of seven, two officers and five enlisted. As the small boat was entering the bay, a wave swamped the small boat and they signaled that they were in danger. A second boat from *Clover* was launched to assist, but they could not locate their fellow crew members or their boat. Further searches only turned up ten life jackets that were said to have been from the missing boat.

All seven Coast Guardsmen in the first boat were presumed killed. They are listed on a memorial in Honolulu, Hawaii for those missing in action during World War II.

U.S.C.G.C. Clover

Sources

www.Fold3.com

The Bellingham Herald 29 May 1944

L.S.T. - 327

27 August 1944 – *Landing Ship Tank -327* was a 327' vessel operated by the Coast Guard during World War II.

While operating in the Normandy Invasion follow up operations, *327* struck a mine in the English Channel. The explosion killed eighteen of her Coast Guard crew.

L.S.T. 327

Sources

www.landingship.com

www.navsource.org

U.S.C.G.C. JACKSON
U.S.C.G.C. BEDLOE
LIGHTSHIP - 73

14 September 1944 – The 125' Coast Guard Cutter's *Jackson* and *Bedloe* were to rendezvous at sea and assist a Navy vessel that had been torpedoed off the North Carolina coast near Cape Hatteras. While out at sea they were caught in a hurricane.

The *Jackson* went down first. She was tossed into the air and capsized under a huge wave and disappeared. Most of the crew of forty-one were able to make it to the surface and into life rafts.

The *Bedloe* went down a few hours later in the cold and heavy seas, her crew of thirty-eight still alive. Most of them were able to make it to life rafts.

It took over two days for rescuers to spot the survivors and reach them by boat. The heavy seas and cold weather took their toll. *Jackson* lost twenty-one and *Bedloe* lost twenty-six.

As the same hurricane worked its way up the cost it carried *Lightship 73* from her station at Cuttyhunk Island off of Vineyard Sound, Massachusetts. She was never found and all twelve aboard were considered drowned.

In total, fifty-nine Coast Guardsmen were lost in the hurricane.

U.S.C.G.C. Jackson

Sources

www.ibiblio.org

www.wikimapia.org – picture of Jackson & *Bedloe*

www.lightphotos.net – picture of Lightship 73

U.S.C.G.C. Bedloe

Lightship - 73

L.S.T. - 66

12 November 1944 – *Landing Ship Tank -66* was a 327' vessel operated by the Coast Guard during World War II.

L.S.T. – 66 was participating in the second invasion of Leyte, Philippines Islands. She had hit the beach near the city of Tacloban and began unloading troops and cargo. After unloading, she began to load army troops to take to Hollandia and New Guinea. Suddenly, the sky was filled with Japanese planes, and they came in for an attack. One of the planes slammed into the aft section of *L.S.T.- 66*, causing numerous casualties as it took out a gun turret.

First-hand accounts listed seven killed and thirteen wounded. But these numbers were confusing since there was a mix of Coast Guard and Army members killed and injured. Of those casualties five of the killed were Coast Guardsmen.

L.S.T. – 66

Sources

www.navsource.org

U.S.S. CALLAWAY

08 January 1945 – *U.S.S. Callaway* was a 492' Navy attack transport vessel manned with a Coast Guard crew during World War II.

As *Callaway* operated in the Pacific Theatre of operations, she was involved in the Invasion of Lingayen Gulf. Like *L.S.T. – 66* she was hit by a Japanese plane, presumably a kamikaze, on the starboard side of her bridge. The results were twenty-nine Coast Guardsmen killed and twenty-two wounded.

U.S.S. Callaway

Sources

www.navsource.org - picture

U.S.S. Serpens

29 January 1945 – *U.S.S. Serpens (AK-47)* was a 441' Navy cargo ship, but manned by a Coast Guard crew. She was initially used to transport general cargo but was later modified to also carry ammunition.

While loading depth charges at Lunga Beach, Guadalcanal she exploded killing one hundred ninety-six of her Coast Guard crew, fifty-seven Army Stevedores, and a Public Health Physician. Only two Coast Guardsmen on *Serpens* survived the explosion. The blast also spared the commanding officer and seven others who had gone ashore.

The blast simply vaporized *Serpens* and all that was left was her bow, which soon sank.

For a really in depth look at *Serpens*, her crew, and the tragedy, there is an extremely detailed website at www.ak97.org

It is still the largest loss of Coast Guardsmen in any single event.

U.S.S. Serpens

Sources

www.ak97.org – article & picture

F.S. - 255

11 May 1945 – *F.S.-255* was a 177' Army freight and supply vessel manned by Coast Guardsmen.

Participating in the Pacific Theatre of operations during WWII *255* was loaded with 155mm ammunition and anchored just off Mindanao, Philippines. Just after midnight she was struck on the port side by a torpedo. The torpedo struck the aft crew's berthing area. An immediate investigation revealed that four of the crew were missing and *255* was taking on water fast. Abandon ship was ordered, and the remainder of the crew made it safely off *255* before she rolled over and sank.

Of the crew of twenty, four were killed in the attack.

vessel similar to *F.S. – 255*

Sources

www.media.defense.gov

www.ww2online.org

CG-32740 J2F-6

15 December 1945 – This is an exception to limiting my chapters to those with at least three casualties. I made this exception because the tragedy involved a Coast Guard Cutter and a Coast Guard plane, which is unusual with aviation casualties.

Coast Guard *32740* was a Grumman JF2-6 single propeller aircraft, known as a duck. It was assigned to the Coast Guard Cutter *Eastwind,* which was just completing a Greenland Patrol and was headed to its homeport of Boston, Massachusetts. As the cutter was nearing Deer Island, she prepared to launch *32740* so it could be flown to the Grumman maintenance facility in New York City.

The following is an eyewitness account of what happened. "Before the plane was put over the side, the pilot would start up the engine and make sure all the systems were working fine. Then the plane would shut down, hoisted over the side by the crane operator and then started up again. The plane was in perfect condition or McCormick (pilot) would never have signaled the crane operator to release him after being lowered to the water.

I was topside on the main deck just forward of the twin 5" gun mount, securing the cover plates on the fuel in/out take lines. Lil Mac (pilot) and Robinson (crewmember) taxied away from the rear of the ship about 100 yards, did a 180 and made a run back toward the ship on the port side. Just as the plane was about 50 yards ahead of the ship and 50 to 75 feet in the air, the roaring engine exploded into a fireball. I was so shocked I couldn't believe it. I practically fell to my knees with shock from seeing the explosion. After the explosion the plane nosed into the ocean and disappeared in an instant. Nothing but small scraps of the plane were found, and as far as I knows, the bodies were never recovered."

USCGC Eastwind

Sources

www.check-six.com

The Boston Globe 18 December 1945

CG-46497 PBY-5A

18 December 1945 - Coast Guard *46497*, a Consolidated PBY-5A Catalina twin propeller aircraft, was transiting from Coast Guard Air Station Biloxi, Mississippi to a final destination of Naval Air Station Seattle, Washington for overhaul. She had landed at Love Field, Dallas, Texas for repairs and picking up an Army member before departing.

Soon after takeoff *46497* experienced mechanical problems with one of her engines and requested emergency clearance to nearby Fort Worth, Texas. As she approached Fort Worth the pilot reported that one engine had cut out and the other was leaking oil badly. The plane appeared out of the low cloud cover, started to spin, and impacted the ground at the Hicks-Ross farm, three miles east of Haslet. Eyewitnesses at a farm near Haslet stated that they did not notice any flames coming from the plane, but one engine appeared to be out.

All six Coast Guard crewmembers and one Army soldier were killed. Some of the bodies were located nearly 700 yards from the wreckage and all were badly burned.

Sources

Fort Worth Star-Telegram dated 19/20 Dec 1945

B-17

09 July 1946 – The B-17 flying fortress was designed as a bomber, but in this application was converted to carry passengers. The four-engine plane was travelling from Labrador, Newfoundland enroute to Westover Field, Massachusetts with Coast Guard passengers.

As the big B-17 made its approach to land at Westover Field it circled once and made contact with the tower. As it approached it slammed into fog covered Mt. Tom, about seven miles from the airport. A diary from the pilot found in the wreckage indicated that there was a problem with the number 2 engine and it had caught fire. This is substantiated by numerous witnesses who stated they saw a fire coming from the B-17 before hearing it crash into the fog covered mountain.

The crash site also revealed several passengers had parachutes on, indicating they may have realized there was danger of a crash.

The multi-page article in the Holyoke Daily Transcript is very detailed, interesting, and has several pictures of the crash site.

Of the twenty-five bodies recovered, thirteen were Coast Guardsmen.

B-17

Sources

Holyoke Daily Transcript 10 July 1946

The News and Observer 11 July 1946

www.fineartamerica.com – picture of B-17

CG-48284 PBY-5A

07 August 1946 – The crew of Coast Guard *48284*, a Consolidated PBY-5A Catalina, was assigned to Coast Guard Air Station San Francisco, California. While returning from searching for a missing fishing vessel she crashed into the Pacific Ocean off Point Arena, California. The impact was very close to the Coast Guard station and lighthouse at Port Arena.

A witness, the lighthouse keeper, stated "I saw the plane as it fell about 300 hundred yards off the shore. As it hit the water, it exploded, and there was a great ball of flame. I heard a loud roar. I directed men from the life station to the scene. They found one body near the scene, and I found another one that had floated onto the beach. It was still strapped in the seat and appeared to be the body of a youth about 17 years old. The plane sank within five minutes after the crash." The lighthouse keeper also reported that he saw a life raft floating near where the plane sank. He said, "It may have had a body in it, but it was getting dark and we couldn't tell."

All six Coast Guard crewmembers were killed, and the cause of the crash was never determined. The missing fishing vessel was later found to have made it to port the day before the crash.

Sources

The San Francisco Examiner 8/9 August 1946

CG-48328 PBY-5A

11 February 1947 – Coast Guard *48328* is another Consolidated PBY-5 Catalina identical to the one in the previous story. She was assigned to Coast Guard Air Station Port Angeles, Washington. The aircraft was headed to a final destination of New York. While enroute to Medford, Oregon the pilot radioed the tower in Medford that he was over Tiller, Oregon in the Cascade Mountains, about 45 minutes from Medford and experiencing strong headwinds. The tower noted that *48328* was flying low for being in mountain country, and that *48328* did not indicate experiencing any problems. The plane never arrived, and a search was started.

Searchers found *48328* the next day. It had plowed into Diamond Rock on Mount Richter, eight miles south of Tiller. Two survivors crawled out of the burning wreckage, one badly burned and the other suffering from shock and exposure. One of the survivors explained that the plane was flying in dense fog when suddenly the mountain appeared out of the mist. The pilot tried to swerve, but one wing was torn off sending the plane plummeting to the ground and bursting into flames.

Four of the crewmembers were killed and two survived. It took several days to bring the four bodies down off the mountain due to the location and weather.

Sources

Statesman Journal 12 February 1947

The News Review 13 February 1947

www.cgaviationhistory.org

CG-45435 PBM-5G

22 February 1947 – Coast Guard *45435* was a Martin PBM-5G Mariner twin propeller aircraft assigned to Coast Guard Air Station San Diego, California. She was on a "Mercy Flight" covering 1,400 miles to pick up a sick crewman on the fishing vessel *Dorothy Lee*. *45435* had to adjust the pickup point due to incorrect information provided to them, causing a two-hour delay. She eventually picked up the pneumonia-stricken fisherman from San Ignacio Bay in Mexico and commenced transiting back to San Diego. The pilot reported that he was coming down through the clouds, or thick fog, for a landing at Air Station San Diego. As he descended over the Los Coronados Islands at about 2230 the plane struck a butte or mesa near the U.S. Mexican border. The plane tumbled and scattered wreckage over 200 yards.

Rescue crews didn't arrive until 0800 the following day and found two survivors, but neither could give an account of what happened to cause the crash.

Nine Coast Guard crewmembers, two civilian students, and the fisherman they picked up in Mexico were killed.

Coast Guard PBM-5G

Sources

The Wichita Eagle 24 February 1947

www.zianet.com – picture

CG-05049 R50-4

24 January 1948 – Coast Guard *05049* was a Lockheed R50-4 Lodestar twin propeller plane assigned to Coast Guard Air Station Arlington, Virginia. The plane had taken off from Newark, New Jersey at 0637 with a final destination of Washington, DC. The pilot tried to land at National Airport in Washington, DC but a driving snowstorm prevented a landing attempt. The last radio transmission was that he was over the Baltimore Airport at 0836, but the driving snowstorm was also preventing him from landing. The Coast Guard said that reports had come in hearing the plane as far south as Virginia and north to Fort Dix, New Jersey. A search was conducted, but the plane was never found.

It wasn't until the 16th of March when the body of one of the crewmembers washed ashore in Baltimore Harbor sealing the fate of the plane. Then on the 19th the pilot's body washed ashore in the same location as the first.

Four Coast Guardsmen were killed.

Lockheed R50-4 Lodestar

Sources

Courier-Post 24 January 1948

Evening Star 19 March 1948

www.avionslegendaires.net - picture

CG-84740 PBM-5G

27 May 1952 – Coast Guard *84740* was a Martin PBM-5 Mariner twin engine plane assigned to Coast Guard Air Station Port Angeles, Washington. She was taking off from the Air Station on a routine flight to Prince Rupert, British Columbia when the aircraft faltered, or stalled, and fell from an altitude of 200 feet into the water a quarter mile east of Ediz Hook.

The nearby Coast Guard Station was on scene in minutes, rescuing seven and sending divers down for the four that remained in the plane. Those four perished in the crash.

The four killed consisted of three Coast Guardsmen and one Air Force Airman. There were seven who survived the crash.

Sources

Pasadena Independent 28 May 1952

CG-46640 PBY-6A

11 November 1952 – Coast Guard *46640* was a Consolidated PBY-6A twin propeller plane assigned to Coast Guard Air Detachment Guam.

The aircraft was taking off from Naval Air Station Agana, Guam on a routine night training flight. Twenty minutes into the flight it lost an engine and was attempting to return to NAS Agana to land. While attempting the landing the plane crashed and burst into flames.

Three Coast Guardsmen were killed and two were slightly injured.

Sources

www.check-six.com

The Macon News 12 November 1952

CG-84738 PBM-5G

18 January 1953 - Coast Guard *84738* was a Martin PBM-5G Mariner twin propeller plane assigned to Coast Guard Detachment Sangley Point, Philippines and supporting operations in the Korean War.

A Navy Neptune P2V had been shot down by Chinese Communist on Namoi Island, causing it to crash in the water of the Formosa Strait. Coast Guard *84738,* with a crew of eight, was scrambled from Sangley Point and arrived over the downed P2V. The pilot made several passes evaluating the water conditions, which were questionable for a landing. He knew the Navy crew of eleven had been in the frigid water for over three hours, and time was critical. He estimated they only had about one more hour of survival left and said he took a calculated risk in dropping down to pick them up.

After landing the *84738* on the water close to the P2V, the Coast Guard crew were able to get nine of the eleven Navy crew aboard. But two in a smaller raft had drifted towards Chinese forces and were captured. The pilot recalled the take-off;

"There was a 15-foot sea and a 25-mile wind. Everything was rolling very well and I thought it was in the bag. And so, I fired my JATO bottles to help my plane get airborne. (If you look back at *CG-45435* you can see a PBM-5G using JATO bottles) Suddenly the plane lurched to the left. I saw the left wing float rise above the sea but the port engine seemed to be losing power. I quickly decided to ditch and made for the crest of a wave with the planes hull. My seat suddenly broke and that was the last think I knew."

Then *84738* slammed back into the sea and broke up. The pilot, two of his crew, and seven Navy crewmembers were able to make it out and get into rafts.

Later that night all ten were picked up by the *USS Halsey Powell (DD-686)*.

All eight Coast Guardsmen were awarded the Gold Lifesaving Medal, five posthumously.

Sources

www.check-six.com

The Daily Times 21 January 1953

www.navsource.org – picture of DD-686

Neptune P2V

U.S.S. Halsey Powell (DD-686)

CG-1303 HO4S-3G

20 January 1954 – Coast Guard *1303* was a Sikorsky HO4S-3G helicopter assigned to Coast Guard Air Station Port Angeles, Washington.

The crew of five were conducting practice operations in the Strait of Juan de Fuca, about a half mile from the Coast Guard Air Station. Witnesses said the small tail rotor flew off the helicopter first, and seconds later the main rotor began to break up. The helicopter then plunged 800 feet into the water.

All Five Coast Guardsmen were killed.

Sikorsky HO4S-3G

Sources

The Sacramento Bee 21 January 1954

www.cgaviationhistory.org – picture

CG-128906 HTL-4

26 June 1954 – Coast Guard *128906* was a Bell HTL-4 helicopter assigned to *U.S.C.G.C. Westwind*. This is once again an exception to my rule of at least three casualties because the helicopter was assigned to a cutter.

The *Westwind* had deployed to the Artic along with two helicopters from Naval Air Station Lakehurst, New Jersey. Once in the ice pack the helicopters were flown every day to scout ahead and look for breaks in the ice. Upon entering Melville Bay, Greenland a helicopter with *Westwind's* Executive Officer (XO) and a Navy helicopter pilot took off from the cutter. An eyewitness account of what happened next is as follows;

"The helicopter was about 100 yards away when the malfunction occurred. It came down and hit the edge of the ice. The lieutenant (pilot) was killed when the engine broke loose and hit him. The commander (*Westwind* XO) got out of the helicopter but was in the freezing artic waters."

The crew of Westwind were able to get a rescue boat in the water and to the crash scene within six or seven minutes. But the *Westwind's* XO was not wearing an exposure suit and had succumbed to hypothermia.

The *Westwind's* executive officer and Navy pilot both died.

Bell HTL-4

U.S.C.G.C. Westwind

Sources

www.check-six.com

www.cgaviationhistory.org – picture of the Bell

CG-2121 UF-1G

14 December 1954 – Coast Guard *2121* was a Grumman UF-1G Albatross twin propeller plane assigned to Coast Guard Air Station Annette, Alaska.

CG-2121's crew of five and a United States Marshall had flown to Haines, Alaska to pick up a mentally ill patient who needed transported to Juneau, Alaska for hospitalization.

While taking off from the water in Haines the plane crashed. Three of the crew and the U.S Marshall were pulled from the crash, with one of the crew dying due to his injuries. Two other crewmen and the mentally ill patient, who was wearing a straitjacket, were not recovered, and were considered dead.

In all, three Coast Guardsmen were killed in the crash.

Grumman UF-1G Albatross

Sources

The Sacramento Bee 15 December 1954

www.cgaviationhistory.org – picture

CG-1259 HU-16E

22 August 1957 – Coast Guard *1259* was a Grumman UF-2F Albatross twin propeller plane assigned to Coast Guard Air Station Brooklyn, New York.

After *1259* had maintenance performed on her she took off with a crew of six for performance checks from Floyd Bennett Field. Witnesses on the ground stated the take-off was normal, but immediately after leaving the runway the plane banked very rapidly to the left until it was in a 90° bank. Another witness said that one of the plane's engines appeared to have stopped as soon as the plane became airborne. As the plane came down its left wing struck the ground, and it broke up and was engulfed in flames.

Two of the crewmembers survived the crash. One was unhurt, the other requiring hospitalization for severe burns and broken bones. The other four crewmembers were killed.

Four Coast Guardsman were killed in the crash.

Grumman HU-16E Albatross

Sources

www.check-six.com

U.S.C.G.C. TRIUMPH

12 January 1961 – The fishing vessel *Mermaid* had lost control of her rudder off the Oregon & Washington coastline, near famous Cape Disappointment. She was crossing the bar of the Columbia River in about 10' – 12' seas when the casualty occurred, and she was basically adrift.

After receiving a distress call, Washington Coast Guard Station Cape Disappointment sent out a 36' and a 40' boat. The 40' attached a tow line to *Mermaid* and commenced to tow her away from the shore and to the nearby Columbia River Lightship. Having trouble towing the *Mermaid,* a call was made to Coast Guard Station Point Adams in Oregon to send out their bigger 52' *CGC Triumph*. And the *Triumph's* crew of six headed out to sea to assist.

As the *Triumph* made her way to the scene, the sea state got worse. After they relieved the tow, the 36' and 40' started to head for shore, where the seas were breaking at 35'. As they crossed the bar of the Columbia River a wave tossed the 40' and she capsized. The three crewmembers were luckily able to escape from under the boat and cling to its floating hull. The 36' slammed into the capsized 40', but was able to get the three crewmembers from the 40' into their vessel.

With a water temperature of about 50°, survival in the water was limited to about 15 minutes before hypothermia set in.

Taking on water from the collision, the 30' vessel decided to abandon crossing the bar and instead headed towards the Columbia River Lightship. They made it, and all aboard safely transferred over to the Lightship, which was manned by fellow Coast Guardsmen.

The *Triumph* in the meantime had parted its towline with the *Mermaid*. As the *Mermaid* was being swept to the shoreline and into the breakers, the *Triumph* pursued her. As she did, she took a heavy roll and capsized, trapping one crewmember inside. As the *Triumph* took another pounding from a huge wave the trapped crewmember was able to make his way out of the vessel. He found himself alone, the other five crewmembers nowhere in sight. Luckily, he was pushed ashore.

The *Mermaid* had been able to pick up one of the five remaining *Triumph* crewmembers but was still adrift. Several more 36' vessels from Coast Guard Station Point Adams came out to try and take the *Mermaid* in tow without luck. The *Mermaid* finally capsized and her two crewmembers, plus the *Triumph* crewmember drowned.

The two *Mermaid* and five *Triumph* crewmen were never found.

52' vessel similar to *Triumph*

Interestingly, the lone survivor of the *Triumph*, a new member of the station, had replaced a crewmember heading out on the call so he could get more experience on the vessel.

36' vessel

40' vessel

Columbia River Lightship

Sources

www.offbeatoregon.com

www.uslightshipsailors.org – picture of lightship

CG-5509 HO4S-3G

29 June 1961 – Coast Guard *5509* was a Sikorsky HO4S-3G helicopter assigned to Coast Guard Air Station Salem, Massachusetts.

The crew of three had taken *5509* airborne for a test flight to check instruments. The air station reported that they received a distress call from *5509* at 11:08, then radio contact was lost. At around that time *5509* was reported to have crashed in dense woods between route 1 & 95 in Rowley, Massachusetts. There were several witnesses to the crash.

A power company worker who was driving by said. "I looked up and something, maybe a man fell out of the plane. The plane exploded and plunged into the ground. It was a mass of flames in no time at all." Another witness backing her car out of her driveway said "I saw something fall out of the plane. I thought it was either the tail assembly or the engine, but I'm not sure." Another witness said "He saw a body leaning out of the cockpit" as they ran towards the wreckage. "We tried to get the man out, but the flames were too hot. Then something blew up and we hit the ground."

All three Coast Guardsmen were killed.

Sources

The Boston Globe 29 June 1961

CG-7233 HU-16E

03 July 1964 – Coast Guard *7233* was a Grumman HU-16E Albatross twin propeller plane assigned to Coast Guard Air Station Annette, Alaska.

The crew of five had taken off in search of a grounded fishing vessel. As they were returning to Annette in the dark the weather conditions were murky with drizzling rain. The last communication from *7233* was a request for Air Station Annette to turn on its landing strip lights. Two days later the burned and battered wreckage of *7233* was spotted in dense woods 2,000 feet atop Dall Head on Gravina Island. It would take several more days for crews to reach the wreckage.

Five Coast Guardsmen were killed in the crash.

Sources

Record Searchlight 06 July 1964

CG-1363 HH-52A

22 December 1964 – Coast Guard *1363* was a Sikorsky HH-52A Seaguard helicopter assigned to Air Station San Francisco, California.

This is another deviation from my three Coast Guardsman casualty requirement because of the amount of civilian life lost in this tragedy.

Northern California and Oregon were experiencing severe flooding and Coast Guard assets were assisting in rescue operations.

The crew of three aboard *1363*, two Coast Guardsmen and a Canadian Navy member, had rescued two women and a 20-month-old girl from the rooftop of their flooded home. After the rescue *1363* ran into dense fog and was being guided to an airfield by radar. The helicopter later crashed into a remote area north of Arcata.

All on board were killed, including two Coast Guardsmen.

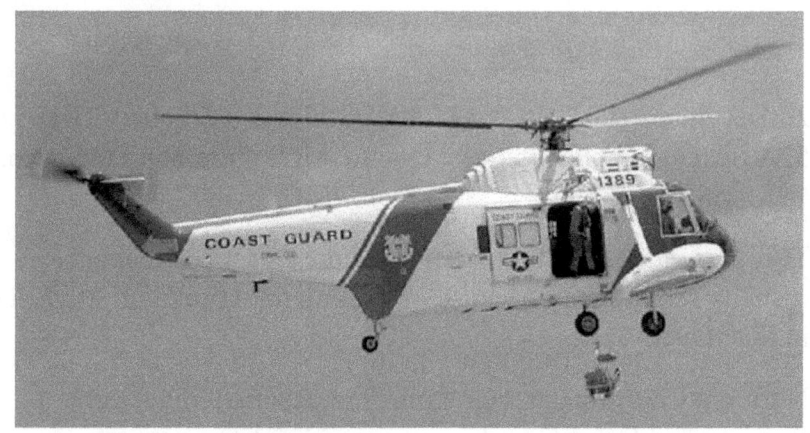

Sikorsky HH-52A Seaguard

Sources

Intelligencer Journal 26 December 1964

The Miami Herald 27 December 1964

www.cgaviationhistory.org – HH-52A picture

Crash site of *1363*

CG-1240 HU-16E

06 March 1967 – Coast Guard *1240* was a Grumman HU-16E Albatross twin propeller plane assigned to Coast Guard Air Station St. Petersburg, Florida.

The crew of six had taken off to assist a disabled fishing vessel. They arrived over the fishing vessel and dropped a dewatering pump to it in heavy fog. But the pump missed and landed in the water. The captain of the fishing vessel said that soon after the pump was dropped, he heard a crash and saw a flare in the fog.

A search for the plane included the *U.S.C.G.C. Juniper* with divers. They turned up some wreckage and found the bodies of three of the crewmembers floating in the water. It appeared that one of the crew had fired off a flare from his life vest.

Six Coast Guardsmen were killed in the crash.

Sources

The Tampa Times 07 March 1967

CG-7237 HU-16E

15 June 1967 – Coast Guard *7237* was a Grumman HU-16E Albatross twin propeller plane assigned to Coast Guard Air Station Annette, Alaska.

The Coast Guard crew of five had taken off in search of a missing plane from Montana enroute to Juneau, Alaska. The plane was flown by the director of administrative services for the Alaska Department of Education with a passenger, his daughter.

At some point *7237* crashed near Slokom Lake in British Columbia. Rescue crews found *7237* and there were two survivors with minor injuries.

Some reports say there were three Coast Guard survivors. But the Tampa Bay Times, the paper I source, states two.

Three Coast Guardsmen were killed in the crash.

Sources

Tampa Bay Times 17 June 1967

CG-2128 HU-16E

07 August 1967 - Coast Guard *2128* was a Grumman HU-16E Albatross twin propeller plane assigned to Coast Guard Air Station San Francisco, California.

The crew of eight took off to search for the cabin cruiser *Misty*, which had sent a distress signal from the vicinity of Piedra Blanca, near San Simeon, California. *CG-2128* found the *Misty* and circled until the *U.S.C.G.C Cape Porpoise* arrived to assist *Misty*. While returning, the plane ran into fog and crashed into Mount Mars near the Monterey & San Luis Obispo County line.

After *2128* crashed, the pilot went for help and was able to make his way through rough country to Highway 1. There he caught a ride to a nearby ranch and called in what had happened. Initially, two of the Coast Guard crewmembers were killed in the crash. Then a third later died of his injuries.

Sources

The Modesto Bee 08 August 1967

Photos from Larry Nudson

CG- 2128 Crashed

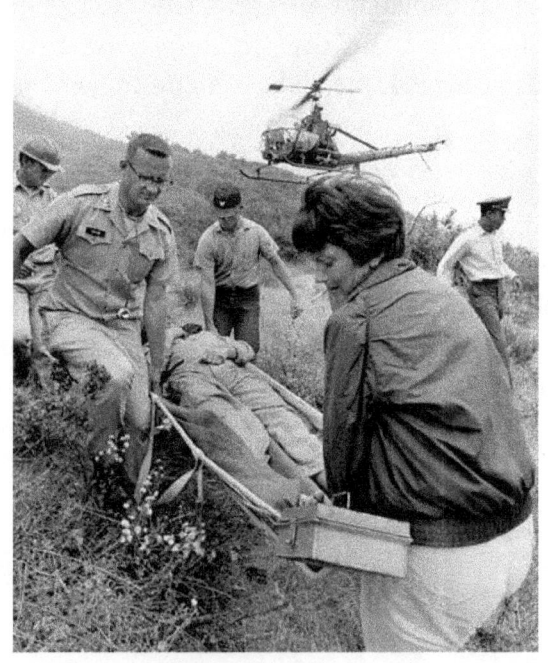

CG-2128 injured crewmember

U.S.C.G.C. WHITE ALDER

07 December 1968 – Coast Guard Cutter *White Alder* (WLB-541) was a 133' buoy tender home ported out of New Orleans, Louisiana and operated on the Mississippi River.

The *White Alder* with her crew of twenty were heading down the Mississippi River when it collided with the 455' freighter *Helena*. The collision near White Castle, Louisiana cut the White Adler in half, and she sunk immediately in about 70 feet of muddy, fast-moving water. The *Helena*, with just minor damage, continued about thirty miles to Baton Rouge.

Three of the *While Alder's* crew were found clinging to a buoy in the cold water. One of them said "I was in the galley when the boat was suddenly jarred. The impact threw me back against the stove. The next thing I knew I was under water and fighting to get back up. In 15 seconds, everything was over."

A witness on land said "I heard what I thought was an explosion. I was sitting in the kitchen at the time. I ran to the window and I saw what I thought was a flare. That's all. I heard a noise; I saw a flash of light."

The captain of the *Helena* said that the *White Alder* turned sharply to port right across his path without warning.

Divers were sent down to look for the seventeen missing crewmembers. After recovering two bodies, the fast-moving river covered the *White Alder* with mud as it lay on the bottom.

A third body was later found down river.

The remaining fourteen Coast Guardsmen were not able to be recovered and are entombed in the *White Alder*.

U.S.C.G.C. White Alder

Sources

Messenger – Inquirer 09 December 1968

CG-1458 HH-52A

26 November 1969 – Coast Guard *1458* was a Sikorsky HH-52A Seaguard helicopter assigned to Coast Guard Air Station St. Petersburg, Florida.

The crew of three had taken off in *1458* to the Pasco coastal area in search of the overdue fishing vessel *Port Richey*. Once in the search area she radioed back her location. Shortly afterwards the pilot broadcast a series of distress calls. Witnesses near the coast reported hearing what sounded like a helicopter losing power, and another stating that they saw a flare.

A search was conducted and the Coast Guard Auxiliary vessel *Diane Lee II* out of Tarpon Springs, Florida found *1458* upside down in about nine or ten feet of water about five miles northwest of Tarpon Springs.

Divers were sent into *1458* and found the three crew members.

The Coast Guard Cutter's *Juniper, Cosmos*, and *Steadfast* salvaged *1458* and loaded her aboard *Juniper*.

Three Coast Guardsmen were killed in the crash.

CG-1458 being recovered by *U.S.C.G.C. Juniper*

Sources

The Tampa Tribune 28 November 1969

CG-1474 HH-3F

16 December 1972 – Coast Guard *1474* was a Sikorsky HH-3F Pelican helicopter assigned to Air Station St. Petersburg, Florida.

The crew of four took off in *1474* to search for the disabled fishing vessel *Wanda Dene* 38 miles southwest of Key West, Florida. The *Wanda Dene* had radioed that it was breaking up and taking on water. When *1474* arrived the fishing vessel was still afloat and their crew of four were hoisted up into *1474*.

After picking up the four fishermen *1474* headed for Naval Air Station Key West where it refueled and departed for St. Petersburg. Regular radio transmissions indicated everything was going as planned as they headed home. Her last transmission was to Bayboro Harbor stating they were proceeding under normal conditions. After missing their expected arrival time, Coast Guard officials sent out a search for *1474*.

Rescue crews started to find pieces of *1474* about twenty-five miles off Sarasota, Florida. *CG-1474*, her crew of four, and four fishermen were never found.

HH-3F Pelican

Sources

The Tampa Bay Times 18 & 19 December 1972

CG-2123 HU-16E

21 September 1973 – Coast Guard *2123* was a Grumman HU-16E Albatross twin propeller plane assigned to Coast Guard Air Station Corpus Christi, Texas.

The crew of six had taken off in *2123* to help search for a fisherman who had fallen overboard from the *Berlin Esther* out of Port Aransas, Texas. It was dark, so *2123* started to drop flares to help aid in sighting the fisherman. One of the flares is assumed to have ignited in the aircraft because the pilot declared an emergency, that there was a fire aboard, and that he was going to try and land *2123* on the water. A witness said they saw the plane make a steep dive, hit the water, and then broke up.

Rescue crews found the tail section of *2123* near St. Joseph Island.

All six crewmembers of *2123* were killed in the crash. The fishermen who fell overboard was later found deceased in the fishing net of a shrimping boat.

Sources

Corpus Christi Caller-Times 22 September 1973

CG-1448 HH-52A

20 January 1977 - Coast Guard *1448* was a Sikorsky HH-52A Seaguard helicopter assigned to Coast Guard Air Station Chicago, Illinois.

Ice was a seasonal problem on the Chicago area waterways and *CG-1448* was conducting a navigational survey of the Illinois River with its crew of three and a civilian from the River Advisory Commission. The aircraft was flying out of Lambert Field temporarily to help assess ice conditions.

As they were flying along and recording icing conditions, *1448* hit two high-voltage power lines and crashed into the river near Florence, Illinois.

A witness said "I never saw it hit the wire, but I happened to glance out the window and I saw a large object about 75 feet above the water. I looked through the binoculars and I could see the top – I wasn't sure if it was the top part, the tail, or the propeller – sticking out. It fell right in the channel where the towboats had been running. I think if it had landed outside the channel, it may not have submerged."

Rescue workers had a hard time reaching the victims trapped in *1448* because of the freezing temperatures, thick ice, and strong currents.

Two Coast Guardsmen, a Navy exchange pilot on loan to the Coast Guard, and a civilian were killed in the crash.

Sources

St. Louis Post-Dispatch 21 January 1977

U.S.C.G.C. CUYAHOGA

20 October 1978 - *U.S.C.G.C Cuyahoga (WIX-157)* was a 125' cutter homeported out of Yorktown, Virginia.

In 1978 *Cuyahoga* was the oldest commissioned cutter in the Coast Guard and operated primarily as a training vessel. On the night of the 20th of October, she was operating at the mouth of the Potomac River where it meets the Chesapeake Bay, with the intention of turning into the Potomac River.

As *Cuyahoga* was heading north it spotted a light on the horizon and thought it was a fishing vessel headed in the same direction, north. The light however was the 541' bulk coal freighter *Santa Cruz II* headed south. The *Santa Cruz II* had also made out the lights of *Cuyahoga* and the *Santa Cruz II* assumed they would be making a normal port to port passing. As the two vessels got close to each other the *Cuyahoga* turned west, into the path of the *Santa Cruz II*. The *Santa Cruz II* immediately sounded its horn indicating that it was maintaining course and speed, and that the other vessel, the *Cuyahoga*, should return to its original course. After no response from the *Cuyahoga,* the *Santa Cruz II* sounded a danger warning of five short blasts.

The *Cuyahoga* still thought that the *Santa Cruz II* was a small fishing vessel heading in the same direction as her and planning to turn into the Potamic River, like her. So, she sounded her horn in acknowledgement and continued her course.

As soon as the *Cuyahoga* realized that it was in danger, it was too late. The *Santa Cruz II* struck the *Cuyahoga* on the starboard side, dragged her for a moment, spun her, she capsized, and sank within minutes.

Eighteen of *Cuyahoga's* crew were immediately rescued by the *Santa Cruz II* and she remained on scene until help could arrive. Eleven others were killed, ten of those Coast Guardsmen and one foreign exchange servicemember.

U.S.C.G.C. Cuyahoga

U.S.C.G.C. Cuyahoga wreckage

Sources

www.forcecom.uscg.mil – article & picture

United States Naval Institute – picture of wreckage

CG-1379 HH-52A

17 January 1979 – Coast Guard *1379* was a Sikorsky HH-52A Seaguard helicopter assigned to Coast Guard Air Station Miami, Florida.

The crew of four aboard *1379* were returning from a training flight over Biscayne Bay to Opa-locka Airport, where the Coast Guard Air Station is located. As they flew over Runway 36 towards their landing pad, *1379* was alerted to another helicopter, a *Bell 47*, taking off in the vicinity. That helicopter was practicing take off and landings.

As *1379* was coming in for their landing, and the *Bell 47* was taking off, they both turned into each other. They collided about two hundred feet above the airfield, and both burst into flames, crashing down onto the airfield.

Rescue crews said they could see the four Coast Guardsmen still strapped in their seats as *1379* burned on the ground. The *Bell 47* pilot was thrown from his helicopter while in the air.

All four Coast Guardsmen and the civilian pilot of the other helicopter were killed.

Sources

Fort Lauderdale News 18 January 1979

HH-52A

Bell-47

CG-1432 HH-3F

18 February 1979 - Coast Guard *1432* was a Sikorsky HH-3F Pelican helicopter assigned to Air Station Cape Cod, Massachusetts.

The crew of five aboard *1432* had taken off form their Air Station, located at Otis Air Force Base, on a search and rescue mission to assist an injured fisherman aboard the Japanese fishing vessel *Kaisi Maru 18*.

After flying 180 miles *1432* arrived over the *Kaisi Maru 18* and were experiencing 30 mph winds and 25' seas. The lone survivor of *1432* stated that "We dropped the rail lines (to determine wind direction) and couldn't get them on the boat. When we moved over to the left to bring everything back up and start over again, we dropped out of the sky. I just felt that it was something that took the very wrong conditions to happen, and we had the worst conditions possible."

After hitting the water *1432* capsized, trapping four of the five crewmembers. Only one was able to escape to the surface.

The *Kaisi Maru 18* was able to recover the lone *1432* survivor. He and the injured *Kaisi Maru 18* crewmember were later lifted to another Coast Guard helicopter assigned to Elizabeth City, North Carolina.

When *1432* was recovered the four bodies of the remaining crew were found in the helicopter. They consisted of three Coast Guardsmen and one Canadian Navy member.

<u>Sources</u>

Daily Hampshire Gazette 22 February 1979

Times Record News 19 February 1979

U.S.C.G.C. BLACKTHORN

28 January 1980 – *U.S.C.G.C. Blackthorn (WLB-391)* was a 180' buoy tender homeported at Galveston, Texas.

Blackthorn had just completed a major yard availability in Tampa, Florida. This is a normal maintenance schedule for Coast Guard cutters and usually takes them away from their normal operating area, depending on who wins the contract to conduct the work.

After completing her availability *Blackthorn* and her crew of fifty were making their way out of Tampa Bay. At the same time the 605' *Capricorn,* a tanker, was headed into Tampa Bay. As *Blackthorn* was transiting, her captain assigned the bridge responsibilities to a junior officer and remained on the bridge. Night had set in, and the passenger ship *Kazakhstan* requested to overtake *Blackthorn*. The request was granted, and *Blackthorn* steered to starboard to give the *Kazakhstan* clearance in the channel. After the *Kazakhstan* passed, *Blackthorn* steered back to port. But in doing so she oversteered and was at this point navigating in the middle of the channel. Meanwhile, *Capricorn* was approaching the Skyway Bridge and steered to port to follow the marked channel.

Normal passing in the channel would have been port to port. But with *Blackthorn* in the middle of the channel and *Capricorn* turning port to follow the channel, this wasn't possible. *Capricorn* tried to contact *Blackthorn* on the radio, but there was no reply. So, *Capricorn* sounded two horn blast to indicate a recommended starboard to starboard passing situation. The *Blackthorn,* unsure of what was happening ordered evasive action, but was hit on her port side by *Capricorn*.

The collision left a gash in *Blackthorn* under the water line, and she began to take on water. As *Capricorn* drug *Blackthorn* backwards, *Blackthorn* got caught in *Capricorns* anchor and flipped on her side. She then capsized and sank in about fifty feet of water in the middle of the channel.

It was dark, *Blackthorn's* crew was confused about what was happening, and within minutes she was upside down and sinking.

Of the fifty Coast Guardsmen aboard *Blackthorn*, twenty-seven survived the collision, capsizing, and sinking - while twenty-three were killed.

I highly recommend reading the Tampa Bay Times coverage on this tragedy which I reference at the end of this chapter. It is a series of very straight forward articles that details the event and the recovery of the crew and cutter.

U.S.C.G.C. Blackthorn

Sources

Tampa Bay Times 30 January 1980

www.cltampa.com - picture

CG-1471 HH-3F

07 August 1981 - Coast Guard *1471* was a Sikorsky HH-3F Pelican helicopter assigned to Air Station Kodiak, Alaska.

The four-man crew on *1471* took off on a search and rescue mission to locate the disabled fishing vessel *Marlene*. They found the *Marlene* and her one-man crew about twenty-five miles south of Cordova, Alaska. The weather was extremely bad with 50 knot winds and 20' seas.

The *Marlene's* lone crewmember said that *1471* tried to lower a basket down to him and hoist him off the boat, but the strong winds and seas prevented the attempt. He said that he saw *1471* "descend into the water near his vessel, at which time he lost sight of it." He later stated that he saw *1471* in the water upside down with two bodies floating face down in the heavy seas.

The *Marlene* was able to limp into Anderson Bay on the north side of Hinchinbrook Island where her lone crew member spotted another fishing vessel, and made it into port.

Two of *1471's* crew washed up on Montague Island, about twenty-two miles from the site of the crash. The fuselage of *1471* and one more crewmember were later recovered. But the fourth crewmember was never recovered.

All four Coast Guardsmen were killed in the crash.

Sources

Arizona Daily Sun 09 August 1981

www.check-six.com

CG-1427 HH-52A

22 October 1981 - Coast Guard *1427* was a Sikorsky HH-52A Seaguard helicopter assigned to Coast Guard Air Station Mobile, Alabama.

The crew of four had taken off in *1427* to practice instrument approaches. Departing from Mobile Airport, where the Air Station was located, they were only about 15 minutes into the flight when they crashed into a wooded area about a mile from the airport.

A witness said that they saw the aircraft explode and plunge to the ground. "I had just walked out of my wood shop; I came out and I heard the helicopter. It sounded like a helicopter, and the rotary blades started making a funny sound. I watched it for a second or two and I seen a big ball of fire come off the top of it and it looked like some kind of flare or something went out from it when it blowed up."

All four Coast Guardsmen were killed in the crash.

<u>Sources</u>

Sun Herald 23 October 1981

Birmingham Post herald 23 October 1981

CG-1420 HH-52A

07 January 1982 - Coast Guard *1420* was a Sikorsky HH-52A Seaguard helicopter assigned to Coast Guard Air Station Barbers Point, Hawaii.

The crew of three had left Air Station Barbers Point in *1420* to search for the fishing vessel *Pan Am,* who was in distress.

After not returning, a search helicopter spotted the wreckage of *1420* perched on a ridge in Wailau Valley on the island of Molokai, Hawaii. The three Coast Guardsmen were killed in the crash and their bodies were recovered.

The fishing vessel *Pan Am* was located by a Navy vessel with her crew all safe.

Sources

The Honolulu Advertiser 10 January 1982

CG-1473 HH-3F

02 November 1986 - Coast Guard *1473* was a Sikorsky HH-3F Pelican helicopter assigned to Air Station Kodiak, Alaska.

CG-1473 and her crew of six took off to make an emergency medical flight to a remote village where an Eskimo had sustained a severe head injury. The crew consisted of four Coast Guard crewmembers, a doctor with the Public Health Service, and a Coast Guard Corpsmen. While enroute *1473* crashed into the 1,050-foot rock sticking out of the sea on Ugak Island, forty miles south of Kodiak. All six aboard were killed.

Sources

The Berkshire Eagle 04 November 1986

The Missoulian 19 November 1986

U.S.C.G.C. MESQUITE

04 December 1989 – Coast Guard Cutter *Mesquite (WLB-305)* was a 180' buoy tender home ported out of Charlevoix, Michigan.

Mesquite and *Blackthorn* were sister ships, built by the same builder, not even a year apart. But unlike *Blackthorn*, this tragedy does not involve the loss of human life, but rather the loss of a cutter. This incident happened when I was serving at sea with the Coast Guard. And I remember the emotional toll the loss of the *Mesquite* took on her crew and the Coast Guard community, as if a crew member had been lost.

Mesquite was racing to work buoys on Lake Superior before a winter storm was forecasted to hit and the lake start to ice up. Lake Superior wasn't *Mesquites* normal operating area, and she was assisting another buoy tender who required repairs. While working a buoy at night off Michigan's Keweenaw Point, *Mesquite* ran aground on a ledge. The rocky bottom ripped open part of her hull, causing flooding. The *Mesquite* settled on the rocks, but the captain feared that the uncontrolled flooding may cause the *Mesquite* to capsize or roll off the ledge. So, he sent out distress calls and ordered the fifty-three crew members to abandon ship. This was accomplished and the crew was picked up by the cargo ship *Mangal Desai*.

Initially the *Mesquite* was thought to be salvageable since it had settled in only twelve feet of water. But salvage operations were halted due to that bad winter storm that moved in. When a salvage crew finally assessed *Mesquite,* it concluded she couldn't be salvaged. After the winter ice and snow melted *Mesquite* was stripped and moved about a mile and a half away where she was sunk as a diving attraction.

Sources

Wisconsin State Journal 07 December 1989

CG-3501 E2C

24 August 1990 – Coast Guard *3501* was a Grumman E2C Hawkeye twin propeller plane assigned to Air Station St. Augustine, Florida. The E2C was used by the Coast Guard in drug interdiction operations.

CG-3501 and her crew of four Coast Guardsmen were returning from a mission and commencing a landing at the Naval Base in Roosevelt Roads, Puerto Rico. The pilot reported a fire and requested permission to land. Just short of the runway *3501* crashed, killing all four crewmen.

CG-3501

Sources

The Daily Spectrum 24 August 1990

www.cgaviationhistory.org - picture

CG- 6541 HH-65

12 July 1994 – Coast Guard *6541* was an Aerospatiale HH-65A Dolphin helicopter assigned to Coast Guard Air Station Humboldt Bay, California.

The four crewmembers aboard *6541* had taken off in search of the fishing vessel *Hope*. The pilot radioed that they were descending through fog near Shelter Cove, about 160 miles northwest of San Francisco. As *6541* descended it crashed headfirst into a rocky cliff, killing all four on board.

One witness at Shelter Cove said, "It was extremely low, they had to be disoriented to be so close over the house." Another said they were awakened by the helicopter, then heard a dull thump as *6541* hit the cliff.

The fishing vessel *Hope's* crew made it to shore safely less than a half mile from where *6541* crashed.

HH-65

Sources

The Press Democrat 13 July 1994

Authors collection - picture

CG-44363 MLB

12 February 1997 – Just off the coast of La Push, Washington, where the Quillayute River empties into the Pacific Ocean, the 31' sailboat *Gale Runner* was transiting from San Francisco to Bremerton, Washington when she was caught in 25-to-30-foot seas. She had tried to make it into a safe harbor, but the pounding waves took off her mast, knocked out portholes, flooded the engine room, and set the *Gale Runner* adrift. During all this one of the crewmembers was thrown overboard, but was tethered to the boat and pulled himself back aboard. Being pushed towards the rocky coastline the vessel radioed a Mayday for help.

Coast Guard *44363*, a Motor Life Boat, MLB, especially designed for such sea rescues was dispatched from Station Quillayute River with a crew of four Coast Guardsmen. As the *44363* was crossing the bar of the Quillayute River at night, a huge wave rolled the boat. The MLB is designed to roll completely over and right itself, which it did, and the crew pressed on towards the *Gale Runner*. On its way *44363* was rolled several more times. On the second roll the superstructure was ripped off and two of the crew were thrown from the boat, the third and fourth crewmembers remained aboard due to being tethered to it. A third wave struck the boat and rolled it once again. The third crewmember was thrown into the water.

The fourth crewmember fired a flare gun at a light he saw from James Island. Riding the battered and out of control *44363* into the shore he untethered himself and waded ashore where he was picked up by a Coast Guard helicopter.

The three crewmembers who were thrown into the water drowned. One was found unresponsive on the beach and the other two floating in the water.

44' Motor Life Boat

The crew of the *Gale Runner* were plucked off their vessel by a Coast Guard helicopter moments before it was thrown against the rocky shore.

For an amazingly detailed explanation of this tragedy, check out the website www.uscg44363.com

<u>Sources</u>

www.uscg44363.com

CG-6549 HH-65

08 June 1997 - Coast Guard *6549* was an Aerospatiale HH-65A Dolphin helicopter assigned to Coast Guard Air Station Humboldt Bay, California.

CG-6549 and her crew of four Coast Guardsmen took off in search of a 37' Canadian sailboat in distress 40 miles off the coast of Cape Mendocino.

The five crewmembers on the sailboat had abandoned their boat and made it into a life raft after waves had broken the vessels portholes out. The last communication from *6549* was that she was descending through fog to look for the sailboat.

After searching for *6549*, wreckage such as a door, helmet and rescue board were found floating in the water. All four of her crew were killed.

The sailboat crew were later rescued by a Coast Guard cutter.

Sources

The Sacramento Bee 11 June 1997

The Park City Daily News 10 June 1997

CG-6505 HH-65

04 September 2008 - Coast Guard *6505* was an Aerospatiale HH-65A Dolphin helicopter assigned to Coast Guard Air Station Barbers Point, Hawaii.

CG-6505 and her Coast Guard crew of four were conducting nighttime rescue training with a Coast Guard 47'small boat, when she crashed into the water about five miles south of Honolulu International Airport killing all four aboard.

Three bodies were initially recovered just after the crash, but the fourth crewmember was missing. While conducting a search in October, a navy crew came across the missing crewmembers flight suit. The body was not recovered.

Sources

The Honolulu Advertiser 24 October 2008

CG-1705 HC-130

29 October 2009 - Coast Guard *1705* was a Lockheed HC-130H twin propeller plane assigned to Coast Guard Air Station Sacramento, California.

CG-1705 and her crew of seven Coast Guardsmen took off conducting a search for a person who fell overboard from their 12' dinghy while trying to row to Catalina Island.

While conducting the search, four Marine AH-1W Super Cobra helicopters from Camp Pendleton were conducting training operations in the area. One of these helicopters collided with *1705* near San Clemente Island, killing the seven Coast Guardsmen aboard *1705* and two Marines in their AH-1W.

A pilot flying in the area said they saw a fireball in the sky about the same time the two aircraft collided.

Sources

Merced Sun-Star 31 October 2009

CG-1705

AH-1W Super Cobra

CG-6017 MH-60T

07 July 2010 - Coast Guard *6017* was a Sikorsky MH-60T Jayhawk helicopter assigned to Coast Guard Air Station Sitka, Alaska.

The Coast Guard crew of four were headed back to Sitka from Astoria, Oregon when they crashed in the water off La Push, just northwest of James Island, Washington.

Fast acting locals jumped into a fishing boat and raced out to the crash scene. They were able to pull two crewmembers out of the water and into their boat. One died after reaching the shore and the other suffered nonlife-threatening injuries. A Coast Guard boat nearby, which *6017* happened to be flying over, retrieved the other two crewmembers, who were found dead.

Witnesses said *6017* appeared to be flying very low and had clipped a power cable that runs from La Push to James Island.

MH-60T

Sources

Tri-City Herald 08 July 2010

www.hlcopters.com – picture

Whitehorse Daily Star 21 March 2012

CG-6535 HH-65

28 February 2012 - Coast Guard *6535* was an Aerospatiale HH-65A Dolphin helicopter assigned to Coast Guard Air Training Center Mobile, Alabama.

While conducting training, *6535* and her crew of four Coast Guardsmen crashed in 13' of water a few miles off Point Clear, Alabama, killing all four. One of the crewmembers was pulled from the water and was pronounced dead. The three others were eventually recovered several days later.

Sources

Sun Herald 01 March 2012

The News and Observer 04 March 2012

ABOUT THE AUTHOR

Ed Semler retired from the United States Coast Guard in December of 2007 with over 25 years of military service in both the United States Army and United States Coast Guard. In the United States Army he was an enlisted man and was honorably discharged as a Specialist Four (E-4). While in the United States Coast Guard he was enlisted, obtaining the rank of Master Chief Petty Officer (E-9), was commissioned as an officer, and retired as a Lieutenant (O-3E).

After his military career Ed dabbled in teaching at a Vocational Technical School and was a self-employed plumber for several years. As a past time, he enjoys writing and playing the guitar, bass, piano, and harmonica.

Fully retired he resides in Schulenburg, Texas with his wife Jana, a retired Air Force Senior Master Sergeant. Please feel free to check out Ed's other books at www.edsemler.com, his YouTube channel at www.youtube.com/@MKCMLT or email him at mkcm378@gmail.com

His other publications are;

"Around The World," a memoir of his 25 years of service as an officer and enlisted man in the U.S. Army and U.S. Coast Guard

"U.S. Coast Guard Cutter Sherman (WHEC-720) Circumnavigation Deployment 2001" which details the *Sherman's* historic circumnavigation of the globe and deployment to the Persian Gulf in 2001

"The Three Gunsallus Brothers" a story about fighting for Pennsylvania during the Civil War

"Sam Houston & Napoleon Bonaparte Meet On The Civil War Battlefield" a true story of the Walker brothers

"Thoughts On Being A Chief Petty Officer" a take on military leadership

"Fighting For Pennsylvania In The Early Years 1763 to 1783 – The Story of Captain Thomas Askey And Lieutenant Richard Gunsalus Of Cumberland County"

"Joe Semler Playing Baseball in the 1920's &30's"

"Alice Springs Australia Adventures In The 80's"

"Count On Us Coast Guard Cutter Dependable – Law Enforcement And Search & Rescue"

www.ingramcontent.com/pod-product-compliance
Lightning Source LLC
Chambersburg PA
CBHW070549050426
42450CB00011B/2776